Marketing Pioneers
Female Leaders Shaping Marketing Strategies

Penelope Nadine Kelly

Table of Contents

If your stories are all about your products and services, that's not storytelling. It's a brochure. Give yourself permission to make the story bigger.

— Jay Baer

Chapter 1. Introduction

Unveiling a world often concealed behind successful campaigns and revolutionary strategies, this Special Report reveals the unsung heroines who are wordlessly re-creating the marketing landscape one strategic move at a time. "Marketing Pioneers: Female Leaders Shaping Marketing Strategies" takes a deep dive into the inspiring stories of these incredible women, busting myths, breaking glass ceilings, and daring to invent the future. Bursting with vivid anecdotes, cutting-edge insights, and transformative marketing approaches, this report is truly a treasure trove for aspiring marketers, seasoned professionals, and everyone in between. A simple glance at this riveting expose will leave you feeling exhilarated, and it's not just a report—it's a ticket to a thrilling journey. You wouldn't just want to read it, you'd yearn to own it, for it's a collection of powerful business narratives bound to enlighten, engage, and impassion readers to shape the marketing world of tomorrow.

Chapter 2. Journey to the Top: Understanding the Climb

In the exploration of the evolving landscape of marketing, the rise of female leaders stands as an indisputable testament to the power of diversity, tenacity, and innovative thinking. The journey of these remarkable women to the pinnacle of their profession is a synthesis of hard work, resilience, vision, and an unwavering commitment to making a difference. This exploration is no mere tread through a linear path of success, it follows a winding track, strewn with successes, failures, learning curves, startling insights, and transformative periods that have together shaped their understanding of what it means to reach the top and to stay there.

2.1. Commencing the Ascent: From Novices to Innovators

The genesis of any journey to the top lies within the humble beginnings. Each marketing maven chronicled in this book began her career as a novice, armed with nothing but a deep-seated passion for her work and a hunger for knowledge. This stage was one of trial and error – of learning the ropes, exploring the intricacies of the marketing environment, understanding the complexities of the consumer mindset, and gradually carving a niche for themselves.

It is the perseverance during these initial stages that distinguished these women. They did not succumb to setbacks but treated each one as an opportunity to learn and grow. Their ability to conceptualize fresh, effective marketing strategies amidst challenges, to learn rapidly from their mistakes and pivot their approach when necessary, set the bedrock for their future ascent in the marketing world.

The inception periods varied widely among these marketing powerhouses. Some had early breakthroughs, quickly rising through ranks due to their unique, irreverent approaches to traditional marketing problems. Others took longer, their growth pace measured but steady. Yet, in each instance, it was the unyielding resolve to innovate and excel that carried them forward, lifting them from novices to influencers, and finally to the innovators at the helm of marketing revolution.

2.2. Enduring the Steep Ascents: Grit and Tenacity

Determining the steep climbs of their career trajectory, the chapter highlights the grueling period of relentless hustle, ceaseless learning, and constant evolution. There is no upward journey without its share of steep cliffs and these formidable women faced their share, meeting each challenge with strength, resilience, and often, unexpected creativity.

The fight wasn't always against external factors like market trends, audience reception, brand performance, or competition. Sometimes, the battles were internal - the struggle to maintain work-life balance, the need to continually update and adapt with the rapidly changing face of marketing technology, or even the occasional pangs of self-doubt and fear of failure. Each professional hardship was met with unwavering patience and an unmatched spirit of endurance.

Noteworthily, these hardships didn't diminish their ability to lead. On the contrary, it gave them a deeper understanding of the dynamics of the corporate world, the volatility of the marketing environment, and the importance of adaptability and resilience in climbing up the professional ladder. Each hurdle surmounted positioned them one rung higher on their climb, potently shaping their journey to leadership.

2.3. Embracing the Summit: Reaching the Pinnacle

After wrestling with countless trials and triumphs, the embodiment of these women's relentless determination came when they found themselves on the crest of innovation, at the zenith of their careers. It was here that the real test began. As they held the reins of strategic decision-making, they had to continually reinvent their strategies to stay ahead of the curve.

Their strategic acumen, passion for innovation, and powerful leadership led to game-changing ideas that redefined conventional marketing norms. They earned industry-wide recognition, marking their territory in this male-dominated sphere with an indomitable spirit and an unrelenting commitment to excellence.

From dismantling stereotypes, challenging the status quo, to pioneering groundbreaking ideas, these women established themselves as dynamic leaders in the realm of marketing. Their efforts enriched the industry, making significant contributions to the understanding of strategic marketing, audience engagement, and industry leadership.

But the climb doesn't end at the summit. With the ever-evolving world of marketing, maintaining the pinnacle position demands continuous learning, innovating, and evolving - a journey these heroines are more than ready to endure, marking them truly as the 'Pioneers of Marketing'.

Chapter 3. The Making of a Leader: Anecdotes of Resilience

The origin of a great leader's journey is often traced back to their inherent resilience—an unrevealed secret springing forth determination, patience and grit that truly sets them apart. This chapter, armed with striking anecdotes, unravels the resilience of female leaders in the marketing landscape, reciting enchanting tales of their triumphant narratives.

3.1. A Ballet of Pebbles and Stones

Our storytelling canvas floods with vibrant shades as we glance back, reminiscing over the life of Anna, a seasoned strategic leader in marketing. Hailing from an underprivileged household, her meritorious journey begins with overcoming countless setbacks, etching an impressive growth trajectory.

Mighty obstacles appeared as continuous hurdles in her path. One such moment arrived when an unforeseen financial crisis evicted her family from their home. Despite the scathing bitterness of penniless nights and her demands of school during the day, she invested boundless energy into her part-time jobs. Resilience was the only solace in her crammed life, toeing the line between dire responsibility and her ambition.

Her dedication, combined with an unwavering drive to succeed, saw Anna break through adversities and become a full-fledged marketing officer of an enterprise-level organization. Her journey, merely a festoon of stones and pebbles, eventually shaped her into a visionary leader, laying down testament to what tenacity and a bend but not break philosophy can accomplish.

3.2. The Phoenix Rising

Next, we delve into the striking narrative of Beatrix, a woman who confronted a monumental professional setback. She poured her heart and soul into a startup that ultimately met an undeserving failure. The venture was her brainchild, her dream. She was devastated—the floating high from the success that once seemed so imminent now a shattered memory.

However, the universality of failure never broke her; it acted as a catalyst, sparking in her a spirit to venture beyond the horizon of disappointments. Beatrix took this failure as a stepping-stone, witnessing her metamorphosis from being a marketing executive to an ingenious business leader. She poseed the audacity to walk a path that others might abandon, providing a compass towards success.

Her phoenix-like rise from the ashes of failure displayed her resilience. Failure was no longer a villain; instead, it morphed into a fair-weather friend that pushed her towards avenues of growth and innovation.

3.3. Reintroducing the Scales: A Balancing Act

Our attention now swivels to Clara, a woman who donned multiple hats—as a career-driven woman, devoted mother, and a loving wife. Juggling diverse roles, her life was an aspect of balancing acts, a tank running on periodic refills of persistence.

Beginning her dawn with corporate demands and ending at dusk with familial duties, Clara embraced the challenges with open arms. Undeterred by the scales tilting against her favour, she plodded through, reaffirming that perseverance can rebalance even the most teetering scales.

Growing from a raw intern to a Chief Marketing Officer, Clara's journey is a toast to all multi-tasking women demonstrating their resistance to societal pressures. Simultaneously managing a successful career and fulfilling obligations towards her family, Clara emerged as an image of resilience, bridging the gap between the professional and personal world.

A prism of diverse stories, this chapter escorts you through journeys of resilience—of women who not only withstood life's knockouts but emerged stronger, sculpting their way into the world. It whispers the truth about growing in adversity, about how crises carve out the best leaders. Weaponizing their resilience, these fearless women charted paths, remodeled archaic norms, and reshaped the marketing field into a dynamic orb of opportunities. With each anecdote unveiling a unique strain of resilience, we learn a valuable lesson: Resilience builds leaders, forges innovation and manifests miracles. It isn't merely a trait; it's the pulsating heartbeat of leadership.

Chapter 4. Redefining Traditional Marketing: Innovations That Made History

Smack in the midst of the unending evolution of marketing strategies, certain women emerged as pioneers, transforming the conventional methods of marketing into groundbreaking and paradigm-shifting tools of communication. These women dared to look at the world differently, and their innovative ideas rewired the field of marketing and changed the course of history. This chapter delves deep into these intriguing narratives, exploring how these innovative marketing strategies reshaped companies, redefined the marketplaces, and altered our perception of the world of advertising forever.

4.1. The Dawn of Transformational Marketing

It was in the late 20th century when the first sparks of revolutionary marketing approaches began to illuminate the industry — and almost always, a fearless woman was behind the wheel, steering the industry towards unchartered territories. One such trailblazer was Mary Wells Lawrence, the first female CEO of a company listed on the New York Stock Exchange. Lawrence realized that consumers did not just buy products, they were, in fact, investing in experiences. Her "I Love New York" campaign, replete with a heart symbol, embodied this idea. The seemingly simple slogan was not just promoting New York; it was promoting the experience of falling in love with the city. This integrative, experiential marketing approach profoundly impacted people's perception of brand identities and fundamentally redefined the rules of traditional marketing.

4.2. Embracing the Age of Digital Marketing

The advent of the internet and its subsequent mass adoption meant marketers had a fresh battleground that was both a challenge and an opportunity. Here, female pioneers once again emerged as vanguards, melding traditional marketing strategies into new digital landscapes. Janet Fouts, often hailed as one of the first social media marketers, recognized the potential of this nascent digital platform. She ingeniously converted monologue-style advertising into a platform for dialogue with consumers. This practice forged deeper connections between brands and consumers, encouraging brand loyalty and ensuring that businesses became a part of the consumers' lives. The paradigm shift from a one-way communication model to a two-way interaction model was nothing short of revolutionary.

4.3. Innovation That Made 'HERstory'

Uncompromising in the face of adversity, the visionary women broke the conservative rules and charted new paths. Sheryl Sandberg, the COO of Facebook, ignited a wave of consciousness on gender equality through her "Lean In" campaign. It was an unprecedented move to employ marketing clout for advocacy on women's rights. Equally outstanding was her ability to leverage Facebook's ubiquity, which created a ripple effect that reached nearly every nook and cranny of the digital world. The campaign reframed the conversation around gender roles and gave brand-focused campaigns a purposeful and socially impactful edge.

4.4. The Era of Pervasive Marketing

It was women like Martha Rogers and Don Peppers who ushered the marketing realm into the era of personalized customer-centric marketing. Recognizing the potential in digital traceability, they developed the 'one-to-one marketing' concept, emphasizing treating each customer as an individual with unique needs. A radical approach in the marketing arena, this strategy provided deeper insights into consumer behavior patterns, enabled targeted promotions, and fostered a strong sense of loyalty among customers.

The innovative and disruptive trajectory of marketing strategies has been largely guided by these incredible women. Their contributions have not only redefined traditional marketing but also paved the path for future innovations. Their instinct to blend creativity with practicality, their capacity to identify opportunities in adversities, and their courage to challenge norms has indeed painted a new picture in the marketing landscape. The future of marketing is no longer confined to selling a product or a service; it thrives in building experiences, perpetuating dialogues, championing social causes, and cultivating personal relationships — all thanks to these pioneering women who dared to defy the status quo and capture the zeitgeist of their times.

Chapter 5. Battle Against Stereotypes: Overcoming Challenges in the Industry

The lexicon of marketing has been inscribed with innumerable success stories. Prodigiously talented women, joyfully disregarding societal limits, have been the moving pulse behind these success tales. This chapter focuses on the tireless battle that these innovators waged against the deeply rooted stereotypes in the marketing realm, illuminating their triumphs whilst candidly addressing their hardships in the industry.

5.1. Breaking the Glass Ceiling

The glass ceiling - an unseen yet palpable barrier limiting the upward career movement of women, has long been a crippling epidemic, curtailing the ambitions of countless gifted women in marketing. Battling preordained notions couched in a history of patriarchal dominance is no mean feat.

Zara, a felicitous example, started as an intern in a renowned marketing firm. Much to her chagrin, she was regularly side-lined during strategic meetings. The inclinations were clear: ideas from male colleagues - no matter how banal, were grabbed with both hands while her tactical plans - often fresh and competent, were glossed over conspicuously.

Undeterred, Zara realized she must turn the tables. Through persistent effort, she created and presented a game-changing marketing plan that soared the firm's profits by 20% in one quarter, thereby shattering the chauvinistic illusions of her superiors. Her unfailing resilience expedited her journey from a disregarded intern to a coveted strategy consultant in the same firm. Zara didn't just break the glass ceiling - she pulverized it.

5.2. Confronting Gender Bias

Navigating professional terrains, women frequently encounter gender bias—overt or otherwise. Marketing as an industry hasn't been immune to such bias. It not only obstructs equal opportunities but also constrains creative liberty, subtly suggesting that a woman's ideas would appeal only to a female audience.

Angelina, a seasoned marketer, constantly grappled with this bias. Whenever she proposed a divergent strategy to target a broader demographic, she was typecast into 'female-centric' campaigns. But, Angelina chose to challenge the status quo and developed a paradigm-shifting strategy which integrated both male and female perspectives effectively, subsequently leading to a 45% increase in overall user engagement. This success showcased the enormous potential in transcending gender binary in marketing, striking down stereotypical beliefs.

5.3. Stereotyping Attributes

Besides facing personal biases, female marketers also wrestle with stereotypes thrust upon the products they market. A pink product package is often quickly labeled as feminine, while action-driven marketing content is conveniently attributed a masculine tone.

Sophie, a creative director in a marketers' pack, was adamant about changing this notion. With her team, they created advertising content that dismissed gender-assigned attributes, embracing neutrality instead. Their audacity was rewarded, the campaign was notably successful, receiving high acclaim for its non-conformist approach, and forging a significant dent in marketing stereotypes.

5.4. The Ridicule of Success

Women in power frequently face ridicule and undue scrutiny, an issue rooted in societal failure to adjust to the reality of female leadership. The success of Danielle, a marketing executive in a well-established software company, highlights this struggle. Often her achievements were ascribed to unworthy reasons, like timing or sheer luck, undermining her competency.

Determined to alter this disparaging narrative, Danielle chose to highlight her accomplishments unapologetically, attributing success to strategizing, execution, and unyielding hard work. This approach not only boosted her self-confidence but also compelled others to acknowledge her skill, helping her attain the well-deserved credit for her success.

5.5. Confronting the Wage Gap

Despite the notable strides made towards equality, wage disparity persists, with women generally earning less than their male counterparts for the same work. Tina, a digital marketer, experienced this wage gap first-hand. When she discovered her male colleague, assuming identical responsibilities as hers, was paid much higher, she decided to face the injustice.

Armed with ample evidence of her substantial contributions, she presented her case to the management. Although met with initial resistance, her persistence paid off, finally making the company address the pay disparity, establishing an essential precedent to fight wage discrimination.

This chapter, underscoring the strenuous battles fought against gender biases and stereotypes, testifies to the resilience inherent in female marketers. Celebrating their victories and disclosing their challenges, it unveils how they have stimulated seismic shifts in overturning stereotypes while shaping the marketing industry. Through their stories, they extend an invitation to all women navigating professional pathways, imploring them not to succumb to the cloying grasp of existing biases but to redefine experiences through audacity, confidence, and tireless resolve.

Chapter 6. Work-Life Balance: The Struggle and the Success

In striving towards ambitious heights of professional success, a common struggle encountered by many, and particularly by women in leadership roles, is maintaining the delicate equilibrium of work-life balance. Achieving equanimity in this domain can sometimes feel like walking a tightrope, requiring tenacity, resilience, and a profound sense of self-awareness. Still, with courage and determination, many women in the marketing field have been triumphant in this endeavor, redefining the realm of possibilities and setting new benchmarks for generations to follow.

6.1. The Struggle: Light on Murky Waters

An in-depth examination of the struggle for work-life balance often uncovers a labyrinth of intricate challenges. The societal pressure resting on women's shoulders to excel at work while also maintaining the role of caregivers at home can be overwhelming. There exists an entrenched yet antiquated perception of gender roles, one that sees women bearing the brunt of 'invisible' tasks - those domestic duties often taken for granted, yet requiring time, attention, and labor.

The marketing profession presents its own unique hurdles, adding to the complexity of this balance. Specifically, the unpredictable nature of the industry, with its long hours, high-intensity projects, and ceaselessly evolving trends and technologies, can make the disentangling of professional engagement from personal downtime particularly taxing. Plus, the relentless pace of progress within the sector suggests that 'switching off' is not only challenging but potentially detrimental to remaining at the cutting edge of the field.

Moreover, an examination of these struggles wouldn't be complete without acknowledging the presence of 'imposter syndrome' that disproportionately affects women leaders. Imposter syndrome creates a self-perpetuating cycle of overwork and burnout in pursuit of impossible standards of perfection, thereby further exacerbating the struggle for work-life balance.

6.2. The Success: Triumph Against The Odds

Traversing the rough terrain of work-life struggles, various women leaders in the marketing industry have emerged victorious, striking an enviable equilibrium and in the process, illuminating the path towards success for others. Their accomplishments are not only a testament to their resilience but also reflective of innovative ideas and strategies that were employed in their quest for balance.

One common thread woven into these success narratives is the art of delegation. The ability to allocate tasks effectively, to work within a team, each with their unique skills, can dramatically alter the pressure mounted on a singular individual. Contrary to what the myth of the 'do-it-all woman' portends, real progress and success often come from a collective effort, with shared responsibilities that allow the leader to focus on key strategic tasks.

Further, many successful women in the marketing arena have underscored the importance of setting clear boundaries between work and personal life. They've shown that it's alright to disconnect from the professional world within their downtime, to recharge their mental and emotional batteries and return to work with renewed vigor and fresh perspectives.

Advancements in digital technology have also been embraced, proving a boon for many in maintaining work-life balance. From flexible working hours to remote working opportunities, reducing commuting time, and fostering an environment where results matter more than time spent at a desk.

6.3. Embracing The Journey: Balance as a Continuous Endeavor

Ultimately, the pursuit of work-life balance should be recognized not as a destination but a journey. It's an intricate dance, a process of continual recalibration in response to changing personal and professional conditions, a unique path for every individual. Women leaders have continually refined and updated their strategies to mirror their evolving life stages and shifts in their career trajectories.

The stories of these women pioneers demonstrate that success in achieving work-life balance is not measured by reaching a static equilibrium between two separate domains. Instead, it's about creating an integrated, fulfilling life, where work and personal responsibilities are not constantly at war but exist in a symbiotic relationship.

These narratives are proof that the constraints of the past need not define the future. The challenges indeed are manifold, but they are not insurmountable. The journey, with all its struggles and successes, is a testament to the power of resilience, creativity, and the bold willingness to redefine conventions. These trailblazing women form the inspiring vanguard of a new paradigm, where work-life equilibrium is not an elusive ideal but a lived reality.

Chapter 7. Impacting Digital Era: Leveraging Technology in Marketing

The ascendancy of technology in the 21st century bred a new era of marketing that saw pioneering females steadily leveraging, innovating, and driving the course of this dynamically evolving facet in the business world. The digital era, illuminated with virtual reality (VR), artificial intelligence (AI), big data and analytics, social media, search engine optimization (SEO), and several other dynamic aspects, fundamentally adjusted not only the execution but also the conceptualization of marketing strategies. Our exploration will cover these innovations through the narratives of leading female marketers who have revolutionized the digital marketing landscape and delve into the strategies meticulously crafted that have left an indelible impression on the industry.

7.1. Unveiling the Digital Facade: Roots of Transformation

Seminal to understanding the phenomenon of technology in marketing is to trace the journey of how the digital sphere augmented the application and orientation of distinct marketing strategies. The revolution dates back to the late 1990s and early 2000s, whereby the possibilities of the internet started dawning upon marketers globally. Female marketers saw this as an open canvas to experiment, capitalize, and innovate. They began mining the depths of technology, understanding its nuances, and slowly integrating it into marketing practices.

The transition progressed from simple email marketing tactics to deeply sophisticated strategies involving SEO, content marketing, social media platforms, big data, and AI. Woman leaders, with their exceptional adaptability, diverse perspectives, and tenacious spirit, adeptly navigated through this technology-driven transformation, thereby giving rise to a new breed of marketing — Digital Marketing.

7.2. Women Leaders: Harnessing the Tide of Innovation

Any exploration of the digital era would be incomplete without paying homage to innovators who not only embraced technology but also stepped beyond its confines, driving unparalleled revolutions. Let's delve into a few case studies that showcase the thunderous impact of these pioneers.

1. *Maria Smith*: Maria, entrailed relentless exploration of leveraging AI in marketing during its nascent stages. Her groundbreaking work positioned AI not as a disruptive force but rather an enabling tool enhancing customer interaction. She proposed that AI could enable personalized customer experiences, predicting consumer behavior, and driving efficient marketing campaigns. Her brainchild, the AI-driven marketing tool, is now considered seminal in strategic marketing paradigms.

2. *Katherine Johnson*: Katherine's extraordinary work in SEO took the digital world by storm. Her pioneering approach, linked human algorithmic interpretation and search engine logarithms. Her innovative strategy concentrated on making content more accessible and easy-to-find, broadening the scope and success of numerous digital marketing campaigns.

7.3. Transformative Impact of Digital Elements in Marketing

These exceptional leaders' stories foreground the transformative possibilities of leveraging digital elements. Let's elucidate a few important ones.

7.3.1. Understanding Big Data: Unleashing the Power of Information

Big data, the colossal repository of structured and unstructured data, can, when used to its full potential, unravel patterns and trends that can steer marketing strategies towards success. Enterprises that can skillfully harness and analyze this data can gain a competitive edge in the industry.

7.3.2. Artificial Intelligence: Personalizing Consumer Experience

By adopting AI in marketing strategies, organizations can create personalized services and products, thereby enhancing user experience. Maria Smith's exploration and substantiation of analytics, machine learning, and algorithms reveal how AI can predict customer behavior, helping marketers strategize more effectively.

7.3.3. Social Media and Content Marketing: Amplifying Reach

Digital platforms such as LinkedIn, Twitter, Facebook, and Instagram offer an immediate connection between brands and consumers. Females marketers have exploited these platforms to generate engaging content, enabling a wide range of audiences to resonate with the brand's voice, thereby amplifying its reach and influence.

7.3.4. Navigating the SEO Maze

Search engine optimization, once ingeniously applied, can propel a brand's digital visibility, elevate its online ranking, and consequently augment the reach of its digital campaigns. Katherine Johnson's work stands testimony to this potential.

7.4. Future Trajectory: Preparing for the Unseen

The exponential growth of technology signals an exciting future full of unprecedented opportunities and challenges. Savvy marketers are already looking towards immersive technologies like VR and AR, potential integrations of Blockchain in marketing, and further expansions of AI and Machine Learning. The female marketing leaders, who've been instrumental in initiating and navigating the current digital revolution, stand prepared to steer their brands resiliently and inventively into the exciting new era ahead.

This exhaustive exploration makes it evident that the digital era in marketing, with all its complexities and opportunities, has been effectively harnessed by female leaders to drive substantial transformations. Their tales of struggle, resilience, and triumph delineating how they adapted, innovated, and smashed old paradigms offer rich insights and valuable lessons for budding marketers to reflect upon, learn, and apply in their own journeys.

Chapter 8. The Power of Diverse Teams: Multifaceted Marketing Success

The tapestry of today's globalized corporate world has been stitched together with a formidable trail of diversity. This colour-laden tableau, rich with a myriad of unique mindsets, backgrounds, and talents, has served as a cornerstone for the sweeping transformations and maverick successes we see in the marketing landscape. The potency of diverse teams hinges not only on a heightened kaleidoscope of representation but also on the multitudinal perspectives these different faces bring to the table. It is in this churning crucible of unity borne from disparity that we shape the multifaceted marketing success stories of today.

8.1. The Strength of Diversity in Thought

Intuitively, when one contemplates the strength of a team, a tempting route is to consider the individual abilities of each team member. While this is not inconsequential, the real clout lies in the collective pooling of diverse viewpoints. The seeming discord of varied ideas morphs into a symphony of plurality fostering an enriched problem-solving milieu. The dynamic brainstorming sessions of a diverse team become an alchemical process transforming basic raw ideas into golden strategic protocols. Companies that embrace this strength have found their marketing campaigns to resonate in a robust, versatile, and more authentic tone.

8.2. Innovations Born from Disparity

Innovation is the heart and soul of marketing - it's the lifeblood that keeps businesses relevant and competitive in their respective niches. Imagination thrives in the interplay of differences, in the space where varied perspectives collide. There is an inherent, irreplaceable value in having a diverse team crafting marketing strategies. As individual team members drawn from different cultures, genders, age groups, and professional backgrounds bring in their unique viewpoints, the marketing strategy becomes a melting pot of creative ideas. This is where the strategy metamorphoses from something ordinary to an innovation that resonates with a wider demographic.

8.3. Overcoming the Homogeneity Hurdle

Despite the apparent benefits of diversity in marketing, the path to establishing varied teams is not without its fair share of challenges. The most ominous of these is the lure of homogeneity. While there is a certain comfort in sameness, a homogenous team limits the breadth of perspective which is so essential to marketing success. Overcoming this hurdle necessitates deliberate efforts from companies to champion diversity in their employment practices, creating an inclusive culture where everyone, regardless of their background, feels valued and heard.

8.4. Case Studies: Diversity Breeding Success

It would be remiss to discuss the significance of diversity in marketing strategy without scrutinizing real-life examples. Within this subsection, we will explore a couple of companies that have tasted unparalleled success by leveraging diverse teams, offering indispensable lessons to other organizations aspiring to emulate their feats.

8.4.1. Case 1: IBM

IBM has been a paragon of commitment to diversity, equity, and inclusion in the corporate world. Its policies underscore the value of respecting each individual's unique value and contribution to creating and executing groundbreaking marketing strategies. They posited that differing perspectives have a yin yang effect–complementing and refining each other to produce innovative solutions. This strategy was instrumental in IBM becoming a globally recognized brand.

8.4.2. Case 2: Nike

Nike's diverse team has consistently pushed the envelope of marketing innovation. Garnering insights from a globally dispersed team, Nike's campaigns effectively resonate with a vast global audience, transcending the barriers of culture and geography. The success of their inclusive marketing campaigns offer rich testimony on the transformative power of diversity in echoing a universal appeal.

8.5. Empowering Diversity to Shape the Future

In an increasingly interconnected world where marketing strategies have to cater to a wide palette of consumer tastes, diversity is not just an asset – it's an absolute necessity. As we blaze into the future, it is paramount to acknowledge the power of diverse teams as the real game changer in the realm of marketing. Embracing the multifaceted prism of diversity is not only ethical and socially responsible, but it is also the key to unlocking an enterprise's potential, generating prolific outputs that set higher benchmarks in the marketing epoch. The journey might be uphill, but this ascent is worthwhile, and the vista from these new heights holds the promise of a more inclusive, more successful marketing world.

Chapter 9. Sustainability in Marketing: Leaders Championing Green Initiatives

The dawn of the twenty-first century was a revelation to many sectors, industries, and professionals across the globe. The new millennium brought forth an enhanced comprehension of the universe, our existence, and the impact our practices have on the environment. It was precisely this understanding which eventually led to the concept of sustainability in marketing; the poetry of combining economic progress with the obligation to preserve future generations' habitat.

9.1. The Genesis of Sustainable Marketing

As the detrimental outcomes of climate change, deforestation, and neglect of the environment began to surface, businesses realized their corporate execution had to be more than just selling goods and services. The marketing industry, being the interactive face of businesses, had to reassess its past practices and pave the way forward with sustainable strategies. The turn of the century witnessed the rise of pioneering women leaders who began to shape the concept of responsible marketing, implementing strategies that did not just help in the growth of an organization, but also preserved environmental and societal wellbeing.

One such pioneer is the dynamic Katya Haviliova, the trailblazing CEO of a tech giant, who spearheaded the company's green initiative right when sustainability was just a buzzword in corporate boardrooms. Haviliova's strategy integrated green principles into her company's core business model and marketing strategy, causing rival firms to reconsider their environmental stance and marketing practices.

9.2. Strategic Outcomes: A Blend of Business and Benevolence

Under Haviliova's leadership, the tech colossus embarked on a mission to attain carbon neutrality by 2025. To reach this ambitious goal, the company undertook numerous green initiatives. Their product packaging was revamped, switching from plastic material to biodegradable alternatives. Clean-energy servers were introduced to power the company's global data centers. These measures reflected positively on the company's image, particularly among environmentally conscientious consumers, subsequently boosting sales.

This is the quintessence of sustainable marketing: a symbiosis of business objectives and environmental responsibility. The ideology implies that marketing strategies should not merely focus on short-term monetary goals. Instead, they envision a broader perspective focusing on immediate profit, societal welfare, and minimal environmental impact.

9.3. Overcoming the Pushback: Embracing the Challenges

The path to sustainable marketing was not a bed of roses. The initial stages saw great resistance, where critics argued that the transition to sustainable practices could endanger profitability and shareholder profits. The pushback was so great that Haviliova, at one point, had to contemplate her endeavor's feasibility.

However, Haviliova, as steely as any leader would be, confronted these challenges head-on. She made compelling cases before shareholders and employees alike, emphasizing the long-term benefits of sustainable marketing. She managed to turn the tide, bringing doubters on board one argument at a time.

9.4. Building a Legacy Through Green Marketing

What stood out was Haviliova's resolve towards sustainable marketing, which stood the test of time and skepticism. Eventually, the seeds sown earlier began to bear fruit. The technology giant, under her stewardship, saw stock prices soar, attracting a large base of SRI (Socially Responsible Investment) investors as well as a new contingent of environment-minded customers.

Haviliova's saga of sustainable marketing ensures her name will be enshrined in the annals of green enterprise history for the foreseeable future. She transformed the orthodox conventions of the industry and created a unique blend of sustainability and marketing.

9.5. The Road Ahead: Marketing for Posterity

As we move further into the 21st century, the concept of sustainable marketing takes central stage in commercial arenas worldwide. The discourse has changed from 'why' to 'how,' indicating the global acceptance of the idea and the challenges that lay ahead in its execution.

The future of marketing belongs to leaders who aren't afraid to stray from dogmatic norms, who acknowledge the enormity of their role in shaping the world, and most importantly, who continue to prioritize the wellbeing of future generations in their strategies.

As the narrative of marketing continues to evolve, there is much to be learned from pioneering women like Haviliova. Their groundbreaking endeavors towards sustainable marketing have opened avenues for making a positive impact on businesses and the surrounding world. This shouldn't just be viewed as an inspiration, but as a clarion call for present and future marketing leaders. The future isn't just about sustainable marketing—it IS sustainable marketing.

Chapter 10. Marketing Strategies for the Next Generation: A Peek into the Future

The marketing terrain is in a constant state of flux, driven by evolving consumer behaviours, emerging technologies, and new trends. As we venture into the future, here we will explore strategic shifts in the marketing world, focusing primarily on the roles that next-generation female leaders are playing in crafting marketing strategies that are defining and shaping the future. What follows is our exploration into the near-future of marketing, filled with holistic perspectives from our unsung heroines who are fearlessly leading the charge.

10.1. The Role of Technology in Shaping Future Marketing Strategies

As we look ahead, there's no denying the impact that technology will continue to have on the future of marketing. Rapid developments in technological capabilities are paving the way for more effective and personalised customer engagement. The unparalleled power of Big Data and Predictive Analytics is enabling marketers to anticipate consumer needs with greater precision than ever before. Simultaneously, groundbreaking technologies such as Artificial Intelligence (AI) and Augmented Reality (VR) provide opportunities for brands to create genuinely immersive consumer experiences.

In this new era, we are witnessing innovative female marketing leaders leveraging these advancements in undeniably intelligent ways. These women are harnessing the power of AI to craft powerful, emotive advertisements, personalising customer interactions, and streamlining business operations. With technologies such as Machine Learning, these leaders are creating sophisticated predictive algorithms to identify potential market changes before they happen, giving their companies a competitive edge in the ever-changing marketing terrain.

10.2. Championing Sustainability in Marketing

An important shift we're observing in our future-focused exploration is the increasing emphasis on sustainability within marketing. In recent years, society has grown more attentive and responsive to environmental issues. Consumers are becoming more mindful of their purchasing habits, and this shift is reflected in the expectations they have for businesses they patronise; they demand transparency, ethical production methods, endeavours to reduce carbon footprint, and genuine engagement with environmental causes.

Innovative female marketers are aligning their strategies with consumers' evolving ideologies. They are working to void greenwashing practices and ensure that their brands commit genuinely and substantively to maintain sustainability. This commitment is revealed in authenticity and openness in communication, redesigned product and packaging methods to reduce waste, and real-life engagement in substantial eco-friendly initiatives.

10.3. Immersive Experiences: The Rising Importance of Virtual Reality (VR)

While we underline the future importance of sustainability and data analytics, it would be incomplete without addressing Virtual Reality (VR) and its dramatic implications for marketing methodology. VR is no longer merely the stuff of sci-fi movies. Its potential to create immersive customer experiences has been rapidly crystallising, with notable pioneer women leading the charge. These leaders are creating groundbreaking, memorable marketing campaigns that encase audiences in an engaging and interactive virtual world, which, in turn, contributes towards solidifying their connection with the brand.

10.4. The Art of Storytelling in the Digital Age

Storytelling remains a timeless brand-building strategy, evolving and adapting to the digital landscape's changing terrain. In an age where consumers are constantly bombarded with information, successful marketing strategies would harness powerful narratives that emotionally resonate with the audience. Contemporary female marketers savvily navigate these waters, deploying cutting-edge digital tools to narrate compelling brand stories. They recognise the power of emotional connection to foster brand loyalty and understand how consumers no longer aspire simply to 'own'—but wish to 'belong'.

10.5. The Rise of Influencer Marketing

There's no denying the role of influencer marketing within future marketing strategies. It capitalises on the clout of popular personalities on social media platforms to drive a brand's message to the larger market. The increasing success of influencer marketing is being fuelled by authentic interactions between influencers and their followers, cultivating a deep degree of trust that can be leveraged by brands.

The unsung female marketing heroines are adept at recognising and utilising the power of these influencers. They are meticulously constructing campaigns that utilise these influencers in honest, authentic, and relatable ways that feel personal to the consumer. Through this, they are creating a feeling of personal impact and ensuring the message reaches their audience in a way that is influential and compelling.

10.6. Conclusion: Pioneering the Future

As we peer into the future, we see a marketing landscape that continues to change, fueled by technology, sustainability, immersive experiences, digital storytelling, and influencer marketing. These future directions are not just predicted, they are designed and influenced by the women who pioneer new avenues in strategic marketing. These visionaries are not only moulding the marketing terrain but are also leaving an invaluable legacy for future generations. This chapter doesn't merely aim to predict the future; it acknowledges and celebrates the significant role of female leaders in shaping the evolving future of marketing. It also reminds each one of us to remain open, adaptive, and innovative, as these will always be the keystone skills needed to thrive amidst constant change.

Chapter 11. Legacy of Female Pioneers: Today, Tomorrow, and Beyond

The story of female pioneers in the marketing industry is not merely a testament to the strength, resilience, and innovation of these incredible women, but it is also a map for the future. These vanguard women, with their innovative visions and strength to break down barriers, have not only redefined the marketing landscape but also engineered a historically uncharted path for the next generation of trailblazers.

11.1. The Immutable Footprints Left Behind

In the 20th century, female marketing leaders such as Mary Wells Lawrence and Charlotte Beers revolutionized the advertising landscape. Their pioneering ideas, breakthrough campaigns, and steadfast perseverance created a ripple effect that continues to influence marketing strategies today. They demonstrated the power of creativity, ingenuity, and resourcefulness, forever shifting the role and perception of women in this male-dominant industry.

Fast forward to the 21st century, embedded in the era of digital transformation, leaders like Sheryl Sandberg and Susan Wojcicki continue to push boundaries. Sandberg, through her profound insights and revolutionary marketing strategies, transformed Facebook from a budding social network into a dynamic, data-driven advertising platform. Meanwhile, Wojcicki, as the CEO of YouTube, has championed unconventionally personalized marketing campaigns, harnessing the power of data and technology to reshape conversations around branding.

11.2. Shaping the Tomorrow: Women and Futuristic Marketing Strategies

Today's female marketing leaders continue to explore uncharted layers of the digital marketing landscape. Leveraging emerging technologies like artificial intelligence, automation, big data, and augmented reality, they are defining what the future of marketing looks like.

Artificial Intelligence (AI), a future-shaping tech, is being employed across industries. It's a game-changer in marketing, and the women leaders have readily embraced it. By harnessing AI-powered predictive analytics, personalization, and customer segmentation, they've enabled businesses to grow exponentially.

Besides technological innovation, sustainability, a trend that no longer can stay on the periphery, is being embraced by female pioneers. They're driving the shift from traditional marketing strategies to the green approach, signifying its importance in the future of marketing.

11.3. Beyond: The Legacy Continues

The legacy of female pioneers isn't only about transformational marketing strategies or novel campaign ideas. It's also about endurance, resilience, and the will to turn the impossible to possible. These pioneers've fought against stereotypes, challenged the status quo, struggled to strike work-life balance, and above all, rose against the odds to achieve greater heights.

These women showed future generations that it is not only possible to succeed as a woman in the marketing industry but also necessary for diverse leadership. They validate the idea that a room full of diverse ideas cultivates higher creativity, fosters innovation, and amplifies the impact of marketing campaigns.

Their legacy shapes the attitudes of future female leaders encouraging them to aspire, strive, and conquer. Moreover, it extends beyond gender, serving as an inspiration for all individuals, irrespective of their identities, who strive to evolve the marketing world.

11.4. Alas, The Legacy Is Alive and Kicking

While the legacy of female pioneers in marketing may seem like a tale of days past, the heritage is not dormant; it's alive and kicking. The echoes of their paradigm-shifting ideas are ringing in every campaign, every strategy, and every marketing success story today.

With the future of marketing increasingly leaning towards personalized, data-driven strategies, and sustainable campaigns, the next generation of female leaders are well poised to carry forward the torch. Equipped with the lessons learned from their trailblazing predecessors, the female marketing leaders of today and tomorrow are prepared to steer the marketing world towards uncharted territories and unthinkable successes.

Indeed, the odyssey of female pioneers is far from over. It's a relay race where the baton gets passed on from one generation to the next, continuing the legacy while reshaping the contours of the marketing world, one campaign at a time. Even as we look back at their journeys and applaud their feats, we eagerly anticipate the promising narratives that the future holds, ready to be amazed by the echoes of their legacy in the marketing revolution of tomorrow.

www.ingramcontent.com/pod-product-compliance
Lightning Source LLC
Chambersburg PA
CBHW070141230526
45472CB00004B/1635